BLUE GUIDE

Also by Lee Briccetti

Day Mark

BLUE GUIDE

Lee Briccetti

Four Way Books
Tribeca

Please direct all inquiries to:
Editorial Office
Four Way Books
POB 535, Village Station
New York, NY 10014
www.fourwaybooks.com
Library of Congress Cataloging-in-Publication Data

Names: Briccetti, Lee, author.
Title: Blue guide / Lee Briccetti.
Description: New York, NY : Four Way Books, [2018] | Includes bibliographical
references.
Identifiers: LCCN 2017029367 | ISBN 9781935536963 (softcover : acid-free paper)
Classification: LCC PS3602.R49 A6 2018 | DDC 811/.6--dc23
LC record available at https://lccn.loc.gov/2017029367
This book is manufactured in the United States of America and printed on acid-free paper.

Four Way Books is a not-for-profit literary press. We are grateful for the assistance
we receive from individual donors, public arts agencies, and private foundations.

This publication is made possible with public funds from the New York State Council on the Arts,
a state agency,

and with funds from the Jerome Foundation.

We are a proud member of the Community of Literary Magazines and Presses.

Distributed by University Press of New England
One Court Street, Lebanon, NH 03766

CONTENTS

Blue Guide I

And Place was where the Presence was
Circumference between.

—Emily Dickinson

The Toothache

The toothache drills a hole
to the suitcase filled with singed clothes

of the woman who died in a crash.
Further inside, a shelf I made

when I left my first country, plank I put myself on
with my wooden doll and wooden dog.

Blue Guide, *Rome, Gianicolo*

The two-person elevator
that smells of pastries makes my lover so close
joy in him is sealed into my childhood.

Days, dogs off the leash bark at fountains' aerial braids of water.

Nights, streets' incandescence through a shutter.

Visiting my first country I am always a stranger

but distance is familiar and light.

In this happiness we build each other—
Renaissance painters laying down their blue skies,
inventing a way to see the world.

Blue, earthly. Human love, my true.

Blue Guide, *Rome, Aventine*

Littered with candy wrappers
& citrus rind, streets
dug to antiquities,
time has an odor

of cat piss. Myself:
arch. Arches
hold things up. Dames of Malta
(they exist) lean

toward the famous keyhole
that frames the Holy See.
They also come to see themselves
in full display:

another evening in eternity
darkens with starlings, church visitors
talk about what they ate, walk arm-in-arm,
some in mink.

Day is a blue bottle,
transparent but closed.
O, say the Romans, *Our city is*
built on broken glass, let it break.

When I bend to the keyhole
I want nearness, place
of visitation, body released—
something like sex, like

a look into you
looking into me.

Box Houses

New York / Rome (Alan)

I.

Weekends only—loading dock
near the disgraced IMF leader's Tribeca townhouse
becomes the floor of a cardboard house

Years—
the cardboard-builder on Franklin Street sleeps in
Sundays covered by a dirty sheet

II.

Soft graphite on translucent vellum—
shiny pencil-dark—

cardboard constructions he sketches under bridges—
New York & Rome—

think
also a structure
that will collapse

III.

Domes of open black umbrellas shelter
box houses in weeds

on the Clivio path behind Santa Sabina's cathedral dome,
its Medieval wall & braced steepness—

as we pass, two men wrapped in plastic tarps nod politely
stirring pasta into a huge boiling-pot—

    pushed to live in weather
ingenious   (facility)

IV.

Alan quips that gorillas & chimps in captivity also paint
given the chance

but the chance is captivity
so when we laugh, we totalize

our kinship—
habitats destroyed

darling human opposable thumbs
in their fleshy nests as we cook

in our smell of coupledom—
        just a millimeter of facial shift

causes alarm—
            fragile   (sheltering)

V.

After they drill through his skull
(the nurse says *drill*) he is alive—

his face muscles work!
but within hours he is furious with loss

& sends me away. Summer
ICU scream

that's when he sketched his first cardboard
Box House ripped open

Manhattan Specimen Days

I.

heat pounds belly flesh (messy & fat)
muscle-guy slices on a bicycle   live snake hunked
on his neck/ hours later
there he is! (downtown & the snake)
traffic louder for the heat

how sweaty you would be Walt Whitman
hips dripping/ beaded brow above your blaze
of blue attention   awe-struck by our city's freedoms   gay couples
openly kissing/   trance-talking pedestrians spewing
privacies/ still/ still/ the difficulty to resist
being owned

II.

Walk with me:

Tree is the root of *true*:

to study nature is not frivolous
cataloguing moths & bees
is not evasion

in New York City   as I walk thinking endangered
habitats I'm freely unmarried walking
with my male companion or female companion
alone in the progressive temperament
of stink-laden Manhattan
past Chinese bakeries "can there be
knowledge of the world?" (Kant)

True (root *tree*)

Gravity
pulls my weight toward scorched sidewalks
(millions of years keep me standing)
a system of thinking
cancels awareness of itself & another journalist
on the deli TV asks the burnt Iraqi boy
what he thinks of American operations—

I think: *Imagination* is not the same as experience
but essential for real information

III.

In film after film, New York City's destruction

signifies the end of freedoms & market aggressions
I am never exempt from
even while walking on putrid Canal Street, the canal
        no longer a buried trope since hurricanes
gurgled up basement drains—
buildings east to west chanting
floodtide below me
evacuation zone
water like plump fingers of deranged men
goosing girls up their skirts

I always expect myself to do something
unless I am
alone in the woods   or walking in New York City
my preferred dream-states

alone/ connected
I disappear
nicely   not upset about
my *I…*
I go in & out of myself
the living world is something I
also make up
though I want to make it true

Sky Notes / Sky Sonnet (1)

, here I am accustom'd to walk for sky views and effects, either morning or sundown

, the sky, with white silver swirls like locks of toss'd hair, spreading

, day-close, an incomparable sunset shooting in molten sapphire and gold

, hast Thou pellucid, in Thy azure depths, medicine for a case like mine?

—Walt Whitman

, clouds gilt-gold, long-moment's spaciousness
, moment, in which I hope
, unwell, his eyelids the color of sumptuous gold summer
, voices from the street: girls joke bravely
, time has the sound of newspapers' ignited kindling
, slap of a prow in waves

, until nature halts (a little)
, we talk!
, spirit-chamber lifting
, no omen, just listening in time's compression

, our breezy darkness, our sleep-snorts and dream-running

, nurse's smile surprises up past wet gum line

, our clasp and holding on

, though I have food and money for escape

Blue Guide II

Then lay upon the fire
  An offering of meal
    And crackling country salt.

—Horace

Recitation

Ospedale Forlanini, Rome

Love and *Think* deserve form, not *count the ways*
but extemporized prosody in the Recovery
Room with broken linoleum as he floats
above himself on a gurney screaming
he doesn't know me, when the feel of myself
in my meat pushes so far in extremity
to survive I recite *like to the lark at break
of day* until relief he lives.

                          The orderly
in Intensive Care's ammonia fumes brings
a plastic beach chair—deep night logic.
Sun—faithful I belong to—rises
blood-orange revealing which Roman hill
Ambulance reasoned us to.

Sky Notes / Sky Sonnet (2)

On the Pratzen Heights, where he had fallen with the flagstaff in his hand, lay bleeding Prince Andrew Bolonski.

Toward evening he ceased moaning and became still. He did not know how long his unconsciousness lasted. Suddenly, he again felt alive but suffering from a lacerating, bursting pain in his head.

"Where is it, that lofty sky that I did not know till now, but saw today?" was his first thought. "And I did not know this suffering either,"....and above all this lofty sky....

—Leo Tolstoy

, years mending (the arguments & mean streak)
, his lectures like lit greenhouses
, dream of watering winter flowers, I

, chastened by disappointments, we
, also his falling
, realists are not enemies of poetry but beekeepers battling colony collapse

, golden stripe up his torso, iodine stitches
, fear (also)
, frustrated into stomping is my beloved's body

, then secure again, mind snug (worn wheel-trough of an ancient city)

, 3 text messages—*how are we?*

, 3 moles (the ones I love) angled on his cheek like Orion's belt

, sky-dark illumined, lofty sky

, animal sounds also

Blue Guide: *Ruins*

Ostia Antica

Shall we invent the human world again?
With palm trees & a river to another port?

Each place is natural history:
Necropolis smeared to buttercups at the *River Gate*

though shoreline shifted centuries ago.
Even the marble torso on a metal rod

sans head, hands, legs—
is alive with ochre lichen in the toga's carved folds,

angle of remaining elbow's v
understood as something offered.

(—Slumped-in from Rome, the man on the metro,
fingers fat-purple from a punch—

rough thread pulling closed a yellow ooze under his eye—
extended his good arm to offer a single wand

of gum in silver paper,
which I respectfully refused)

• • •

Vaulted grain warehouses;
crates stacked with amphora & cornices sized

by tens of thousands of shards—
mind manages itself.

The Romantics also made gardens into secret rooms,
pseudo-ruins dripping honeysuckle & vines—

built-image of memory
melancholy but not truly a mess.

• • •

Inside, in cellule, in
earthly time in us,

the mithram's built-dream is not odd:
thank you (unconscious) for space-time in its storehouse

of tile & spilled walls, its Seven Steps for initiates.
Every age has formulas

for self-help & that's what I like
(central basin where the animal's throat was cut).

Fascists in a hurry for their Empire
dug open Ostia hoping to force history

to fetch like a slave—
their favorite, (poor) Hercules

is a gigantic ham-hock & lucky charm
balancing an elbow on his knee like a thinker

his headless neck marked by a wad
of chewed blue gum.

Past is always mediated by present. Did I imagine
or read that disobedient slaves

had their eyes stitched closed
ablaze in infection?

• • •

In the fugitive human presence, I am a ghost
in minor warehouses

(hours of sulfur butterflies).
Who imagined this future

& its permissible
ideas?: invented woman

both free & owned,
stunted by office work, loved,

but childless. The future is
a long time ago—& I cannot consent

to seeing myself as expression
only of species (though true).

Place I return to: "I" "cranial" "actual"
(temporary) with staggering freedoms of motion.

The other world
is always around me:

Messenger
shiny & malign as a modern oil spill

disturbs time at the wrecked Cardo Maximus
in a reality so aggressive

my mind seizes
banishing him with Christian prayer.

• • •

No one walks as far as the Temple of Attis & foreign cults
of open rooms in derelict mulberry

of birds that slue & ruffle their r's
(Domus of Clackering)

of warbler-snap bright as a nail clipper.
Afternoon on a hinge:

I rest in my lovely zone, round C
of the Roman alphabet in carved public inscriptions,

syrup-glug
of traffic, a hundred years, cupped hundreds,

whistle, then rattle-back
of spring's slurp like an oxygen tank—

the dead
always tell us *live*

• • •

Ostia Lido, coast

A dump in every direction—
tarry sand, bottles, tampons, shattered

fiberglass rope. Shuttered cabanas (thick paint
on splinters) stake the sluice of civilization—

waves hurl down brown,
air tastes wrong

but Italian couples on the boardwalk
expect their fried squid & clams.

Farther up the rind of beach, three men, *extracomunitari*,
wheel round—I'm following too close—

past the library named for Elsa Morante & bunkers
for clandestine workers & refugees—ripped bed sheets

tacked for shades—
toward a makeshift Islamic Center

where gold-leaf calligraphy & a flaking crescent moon
announce another tide of prayer

• • •

Ostia Borgo, stazione

Behind a closed shutter, a child skipping
makes interior space deep. RAI news is ground-base

for a baritone who sugars his public voice
behind Ostia Bar's beaded curtain.

The Ancients invented beaded thresholds
to keep out flies   *musca domestica*   shit-eaters

stable enough to imply continuity, though this also is false:
salt marshes gone, Papal seat to Avignon, triumphal & useless

even the Medieval fortress is a huge empty barrel
since the Tiber changed course.

Looking from a window onto a garden
that no longer exists, St. Augustine & Monica

went beyond Time in ecstatic conversation,
released in God's radiance—

where do "I" travel beyond mind?
I mean, what I think the world is?

———————

To be different—in a world which
is indeed guilty—means not to be innocent…

—Pier Paolo Pasolini

Biophilia

And blue broke on him from the sun,
A bullioned blue, a blue abulge . . .

—Wallace Stevens

County Planning, 1977

The Thirty-year Flood predicted
by Army Corps of Engineers flattened
over Main Street past the diner
where old-timers would have

gathered if water hadn't
erased roads. Ooze of motor oil
in sopping fields—March milk sky—
barns pumped

dirty water my first day, first
real job. I walked
drenched second-growth,
made myself by looking, wrote

land-use surveys. Once a buck,
antlers in velvet, charged
& I fell back laughing. I lived
on that laugh, trekked to Agway where the Delaware

smacked through cleared land
& every few weeks a cop stopped
to ask was I stealing
cinder blocks.

Dream Street agribusiness swallowed
dairies whole—even my splintered
rooming house, decrepit raft
of feed & manure,

sold.   I wouldn't last.
In deciduous orange of flood-singe
that fall, they had me drive every
county road to map outbuildings

—lost
I used lostness (or thought so)—
reversed miles on a dirt road
for thousands of butterflies

dimming
way the hell—
some Cat Hollow or Stone Ridge—
where the farmer with a rifle

wanted me scared: *Only Jehovah's Witnesses*
get this far. Winter affixed
its grey metal lid.
The woman's body

dumped up-county
instructed me

Biophilia

The purple crocus pushes through snowmelt
charming & fresh. But nature
is also a wild spat of cells
on my earlobe—let's hope
that can be removed.
Accepting flowers' abundant adjacencies,

I also accept pink eye, the cloud forest
alive with yellow-eared
parakeets irreplaceable
in living dependencies
& the mosquito
siphoning her warm blood meal

on the wide sofa of my
mammalian thigh, evolved
over millions of years.
Elegant, messy, antigen-mystery,
I rejoice in specificity.
Observation is witness

to affiliation—so let's catalogue
earth's insects & the sticky Venus flytraps
insects fall into. We still don't know

our planet, our fucking species
(spooning & licking) (consuming & sobbing)
though shared knowing was supposed to be

Sapiens:

        cognition ablaze—beautiful *derelict*

imagination

Some Insects I Know:

Honey Bee   Cecropia Moth   Northern Walking Stick   Termite   Red Bluet   Scarlet-and-green Leafhopper   Differential Grasshopper   Low-flying Amber-wing   House Mosquito   Fungus Gnat   Sphinx Moth   Green Lacewing   Red Ant   Green Bottle Fly   Deer Fly   Yellow Jacket   Rosy Maple Moth   Katydid   Eastern Milkweed Bug   Brown Darner   Red Skimmer   Green Darner   Hawk Moth   Japanese Beetle   Twelve Spotted Skimmer   Firefly   Pearl Crescent   Horse Fly   White Admiral   Mourning Cloak

Conversation with Question Mark

for Wu Wei

Humming birds, buzz &
breeze of them, straight
at each other like diminutive
saloon girls in a brawl: aggression

in all, in layered turf
& warning clicks as I
sweep the porch. Porches
recreate tree lines

first hominids fledged from,
line of lookout
& escape, says my architect-friend from China
who hid

on The Day of Tree Cutting
in mustard smogs
of her city, Nanjing. She tells me
she wanted her Green-Building class to

sketch trees—bark-bent grandmas,
old-lady-knuckles—
line-planted trees
are human architecture—

but a student-informer
had her stopped. My hero George Oppen
reviled poetry about trees
I say, I think he meant beauty

cannot save us, be alert
to uses of aggression
& fear. My friend doesn't know
my American poet

but if we live on one planet
(we *do* she says) a new
generation must learn to love
trees! Just then, a beat-up Question Mark

butterfly zags to the porch—
miraculous punctuation—
tiny white-painted curl
on each outer brown wing edged

lavender like fields at dusk.
We are on our knees
stained with pleasure
as it pumps open, brilliant orange

Jermain Hill Farm, 2015

Body of earth,
our body—river soil
effulgent Hudson silt,

corn in Eastern light—
a wolf near barbed wire
narrows toward the calves

until Jeremy shoots to scare.
He swears *wolf.*
Language is also tilled

habitat; ruck and pestering
bulb of place through which I vowel-forward:
Oh hell *no* then *hello* Jeremy hollers

as his boy realigns electric
fences he can't touch
because he's sewn up

with metal plates from
the baler accident—
hurt so bad

they flew him to Boston
in a helicopter.
Body of splendid

shattering. Day shines the boxed
pastures. Night—
cut lines of field grass

are fragrant
belts, long sentences,
unclasped

One can say of language that it is
potentially the only human
home.

—John Berger

Jermain Hill Farm, 2016

And Place was where the Presence was
Circumference between.

, belonging to a place, heat-smell, fields in summer stubble (*belonging to*)
, tractor rattles, the fox flushed out
, looking at me—fox

, as I cut through second growth forest to
, worn gravestone of Comfort Ellis, by the giant oak, border tree from
       colony days
, fox, grant me my wishes

, good health; to go further with people; to go further in work
, who knows, someone stopped here looking for Underground Railroad caves
, my Tree in open field of sky, then

, body I look through (surprised by fox)
, once 7 people worked this farm as slaves
, *belonging* (not to themselves)

, yesterday, that shadow—helicopters searched back fields—slicing-
       circumference
, place, memory-bound

Dream Logic

What I wanted: intimate individuals
& transcendent God. Cat
on the mat for a reason. Cosmos, which exits
with its why.

All my breathless bitchiness
balanced by a principled identity:
A cannot be not-A. He is always A
with his life-vigor.

When Alan yells in his dream
"Lee! 1 + 1 = 2! Put it in the window!"
we wake up laughing,
hoping we mean something—

      Love our new creation
      Time breaks into fragments

Life as To-Do List

...writing was in a sense invented largely to make something like lists....

—

Before writing was deeply interiorized by print, people did not feel themselves situated every moment of their lives in abstract computed time of any sort.

—Walter Ong

1. Why live as a to-do list?

    a.   No choice

    b.   I cannot otherwise be multiple

    c.   Lists exist because of writing

        c. is the answer: C is Sun in Cup of Sky

        body squinting pleasure

        (C my cup size)

        monumental Roman C

        engraved on the plinth of The Association of Flute Players

        praising Augustus

2. Why not in-dwell?

a.   No inner space

b.   By doing: measure: parcel: I: myself:
       (contain)

         b. is the answer: b my little Phoenician house
         transformational Busty B
         from Roman floor plans of grand houses

         (prodigal implement
         this life of increment)

3. Transcendence?

a.   aspirational

         a. is the answer: my alphabet
         between dotted blue lines my little ones

         a from Latin alpha
         and 5th century inky hands of Irish monks

indefinite *a* implying a world of others

Apollo god of song above all
all of the above

MY LIFE
~~My Life~~

Field Study

for Marie Ponsot

Attention and the orange bird
make their lyric dash
to bivouac
in waxy-green

further off. (Distance her own body has become—
softened upper arms—old girl
Romantic in grass to the hip.)
She aims field glasses

at mortal music
that bursts into form:
blue damselflies on goldenrod,
red-winged blackbirds—those gigolo birds—

that sputter and whistle
as if a movie star blazed by.
Being and sex,
especially sex, in mind,

which is body
in raiment
of the transitive:
she refocuses

her prerogatives to far away
girls—in a different
life-world and idea of everything—attacked
because they go to school.

Lost

—lost
I use lostness (or think so)—
reverse miles for thousands of
butterflies dimming

on a dirt road—
way the hell—
some Cat Hollow or Stone Ridge—
where the farmer with a rifle

wants me scared: *Only Jehovah's Witnesses*
come this far. Winter affixes
a grey metal lid.
The woman's body

dumped up-county
instructs me

Face of North America

At last, the present.

—Thom Gunn

Face of North America

Revelation Book, 1976

I have known I saved this notebook
        surprised 40 years later
I *do* recognize her

—that girl, her feared body, her Jesus-trail

green ballpoint, unsteady Jesus-script:

Fear is a message—

When I am afraid I put my trust in—

Beautiful, cold night—

Moraine Campsite, packed in hard—

Blue columbine! Praise Him—

Cub Lake, another storm—

When I am afraid I put my trust in—

Farb says all species change the world, but the Earth cannot keep up with us—

•

Face of North America, by Peter Farb (1968 edition)

Continental Divide's perfect suspension

                           drops of water

                                        East

    West

from snowdrifts and glaciers of Colorado Rockies
flare river systems: I underlined:
Missouri to Mississippi; tributary Snake to Columbia

                   grasslands and mesas
sheer rock faces' ribbons of sandstone and shale—orange, yellow—
                  organic matter darker

              First Checklist (I underlined):

Glacier Park: 60 glaciers, retreating ice
Rocky Mountain Park: alpine meadows, 700 species of wildflowers
Black Canyon of the Gunnison: ancient granite, inky depths

...youthful river expends its energies cutting downward in its bed...mature river widens its banks...

True! written in the margin

•

In what I call my Revelation Book

radiation from Time's beginning

pulled through buttonwood trees, grain elevators, the deranged

woman in a Denver YMCA (exactly my age

the year I traveled) who spoke prophecies,

yellow light around yellow eyes.

I took the Greyhound Bus (north/south) migrations plotted

with a pocket copy *New Testament*

and my *Face of North America*, a geological history.

I breathed-in stories—just-released

prisoners, escaped pregnant girls—

in laundromats, on desert plateaus

I was so dangerously open

people talked to me.

In my Revelation Book

old men in cheap hotels knocked just to see me,

young. (I studied them too.)

A bus driver pointed to barracks

where we put the Japs during the war

talking so casually—Heart Mountain—

how had I been alive, not knowing?

But my real life began—

by the glacier tarn hiking higher

on the sunburnt crust of ice-flow

where cold smelled cold

like earth's archive of ancient water.

Each day—freedom.

A handsome backpacker stopped me as I read

The Book of Revelation at a cairn,

sneered *go home*, wiping his mouth:

Courage finds the spiritual path

while staying in the world. Then he disappeared

into an aphasia of lupine.

I wanted to tell him my Revelation Book

was no prophecy of End Times

Listen!

but a wish to be present with everything

alive that ever lived.

Prone in my sleeping bag

months without a tent

at campsites of my country, I woke to strangers dreaming. Darkness,

hugely above me

yellow eyes—

the full-grown deer.

Moist black nose, mist of her mouth,

brown-yellow light—

mystery will find us.

•

In beginning, a black bear (wet fur-smell, Underworld)
snuffled gigantically-by,
I slept exposed—
                        I learned.
Estes Park, the woman architect packed a tent

her fear alive like rushing water
        (—as a child lost in Minnesota woods,
all night they called her—)

she taught me:
national parks *only*,
groups of men *never*,
out-think fear.

•

Greyhound Bus Pass

My dissociative state (conversion).

It was the US Bicentennial: red, white, etc.

Green—I bought travel insurance.
Tennessee Williams-west—streets flashed television strobes

night of presidential debate:
a man threw clothes from a second story window as we passed,

a woman rushed to a pickup truck.
I met a girl (Christian witness) who bribed me with food

to the commune where she unloaded her inheritance.
I got away. Lonely

Main Streets like sunken faces with bad teeth.
Every time I go to a Ladies Room in a bus station

I know I still live
because I did not ride in that man's car.

•

Heart Mountain

Heart Mountain's peak: 10,767
people

one of 10 concentration camps / Japanese Americans /
from West Coast Exclusion Zones /

nine guard towers / barbed /
wire / between Cody and Powell /

8,123-foot high limestone klippe /
remnant of ancient seas /

550 to 350 million years old /
atop younger strata / called the *Basement Granite* /

See: period of mountain building / 50 million years ago /
See: *Executive Order 9066* / 1942 /

•

Revelation Book, 1976

Finally, my body makes sense, walking is reason itself—

Tension to find a place to stay—

The man with blue eyes came by my campsite, said he had four daughters,
        could protect me from his friends but only one night—

Another mistake. No food, no people, only a cement dinosaur on a playground—

In Glacier, ex-pastor said he had a new Religion: Tolstoy—

Told me Japanese prisoners at Heart Mt. learned how to skate—

Aqua-shine of glaciers, Holy Spirit of ice!—

I want to see the human face—

Men of power must see—

There is enough waste already—

•

At the tundra line, packed into billowing, the philosophy professor from
      Michigan
outlined a book on love he wrote forty years later.

Elegant midnight-blue fountain ink
his reading list's steady cursive:

Flannery O'Connor
Martin Buber
Stories of Anton Chekov

my tiny stove pearled its gas jet:

      thrill
      thrill

Years . . . his own books on my Religion shelf, signatures
increasingly crabbed

•

Face of North America, by Peter Farb (1968 edition)

Oh, cunning wreck liquid rock the throat

> *volcano forms a crust*
> *lava extruding upwards*
> > *into vertical cracks*
> *heaved materials*
> > *via wind to cinder fields*
> *speckled in-season with little flowers attracting*
> > *butterflies*

Second Checklist (I underlined):

Yellowstone: 3,000 geysers, canyon of the Yellowstone
Grand Canyon: biggest water-chiseled hole in earth
Yosemite: hanging waterfalls, remnant basalitic flow

...a warming trend is responsible for the march of birds and mammals across
> *the continent...*

> *What about planet's rights?*
> in the margin (green ballpoint)

•

Pink-cinnamon plateau
outside Yellowstone my distant relation
(shaved his Italian name from its vowels—)
let his youngest take me up backcountry

with horses
or walked with me himself in sagebrush
(home from the plant) on scratched-out
cattle roads

under blunt blue sky.
He escaped (his mother and the East) *to live in weather.*
As we walked facing Heart Mt., a prairie dog clamped onto his boot heel
so fast—he pump-kicked high to shake it off

       I asked. He didn't know.
       Heart was good hunting…antelope

•

Heart Mountain

Jackpot for Wyoming construction crews—
wooden barracks were built in six weeks

then heaved huge gaps—

      newspaper-stuffed-cracks / summer dust storms in /
winter-cold / sub-zero below /

      this long scouring:

1924 California Alien Acts
      limited land ownership   & citizenship—

1941 Exclusion Zones
      rode fear   & opportunity—

                                            (they—

had ten days to sell

homes
businesses
cars

gold

    cut-rates

        rounded up, two suitcases apiece)

    we obeyed then

•

        Greyhound Bus Pass

           Wilderness I come from: *how to know.*

at the station (waiting), lean blond
    said he was a preacher

well-spring said
    face pulled over his face

    (hid looking)
blue eyes liquid   the way water *will in*
    ceaselessly will

trouble a fissure

    something calculated—

    fear is a gift   *well-spring*

I was delirious
for attention so I didn't know at first he was hunting

  •

        Gush I was, pebble-wash filling.
             No interest in cities, only

        openness, altitude (remove).

Up Thompson Creek   water-wall's
flash flood gigantic kitchen knife

made banks steep
where fresh guts of houses hung

rain again (they were scared)
(my new friend taught his dog an orange trick)

they let me stay
—droplets sparkled bent flowers

birds whistled-up like flocks of plates
dead sparrow (counted)

(under-feathers grey-purple)
(under-thunder) more rain

they let me stay again because I was a gift
to the father who flirted (and mocked me)

•

Greyhound Bus Pass

A woman confessed in the dark:
her newlywed daughter lives in her home

but when laughter splashes from the young couple's room
she grinds with jealousy—

(*laughter* not sex).

•

Heart Mountain

500 square miles of limestone lurched and slid
as volcanoes lifted sockets of rock

pouring boulders & pressurized water
from the Beartooths in 30 minutes

See: Heart Mountain Detachment (50 million years ago)

Question 27 of the Loyalty Oath asked detainees if they
would serve The United States.

Question 28 if they would foreswear
The Emperor and Japan.

I was deported from my home state without due process of law—
I am detained within barbed wired fences by force—

63 men refusing induction
were tried, transported from camp to federal prison—(insult, injury)

I wanted to find out. I asked librarians.
They didn't know.

•

Greyhound Bus Pass

Wearing down, I called home

Red rock fins, uplift
wearing down

level stockyard's shit-blood-smell
(cattle closed)

a single trailer on graded shambles
—pink bicycle on its kickstand

—pink streamers
—a girl in the smell

•

Greyhound Bus Pass

Hummingbirds sipped at a red fire plug
then an American flag's red stripes.

Las Vegas bus station: the driver of Elvis's private bus unloaded
stories about junkies, showgirls. I could ride along

if I said I was his fiancée.
As I bent to smell roses in chemical fertilizer, the casino

wafted burger-grease—
exactly then, a car passed,

windows rolled down in radio-halo
and boisterous howl and I knew where I was

•

Revelation Book, 1976

From the moment Jesus spoke, the servant began to mend—

Living for ecstatic upwelling of joy—

Praise God, waterfalls windswept to tatters—

Jim and Ruth fed me boiled potatoes and peas. I recited psalms—

What I do next is how I make my life—

Ecological lives give resources (material and spiritual)—

I touch the rock face, pray to live for justice—

Farb says once a wilderness is destroyed, it is gone forever—

I see the fat bug struggling on the skin of water—

I see the earth as living creatures—

This is how Time feels, my lucky molecules—

Recognition Scene

Because the known and the unknown
Touch,

One witnesses—.

—George Oppen

Plot

Marvels of destruction stabilize distance:

Sophocles's storyline: Oedipus is unknown to himself

unable to hear Voice of Gods in Voice of the People

as Chorus warns Time ruptures Siracusa's ancient

gleaming theater—tickets 10 Euros each bought

at the Mouth of Dionysius for an otherwise humdrum

staging that transforms Chorus's admonitions

to high frequencies broadcast by synthesizer

beyond human hearing through the open stadium

so that neighborhood dogs bark at the threshold

of perception whenever Chorus declaims

its inscrutable commentary

turn

turn around

Exclusion Zone

Chambers Street, New York City

I.

blond teenagers pray at the wrong construction pit
      steel ribbing whacks
muddy fundament

girl-tourist with seeping blue mascara cries *Jesus*
      I say: *you're mistaken—*
go three blocks south—

      pilgrimage enacts body-thinking
in time   memorial walls & wreaths
                    (picnic tables to the side)

so much to remember   (WWII monuments crumble)
memory   easily makes
      a liar—

gleaming
      resilience

fear & sales
of my neighborhood

—burn

they slipped through

—screaming

II.

from the well
of my body
dream of oilrigs
on Chambers Street rooftops

drills with iambic
regularity to feed on
murderous impulses:
I am a stored-thing

of dark liquids
hospital bed attachment &
thinking-I
high in the mind's compartment—

if only my real eyes
were open
I would warn
sleeping neighbors:

people are changed
        people are fuel

III.

mind escapes
by getting smaller—*we live here*

this is a city—I yell backward into injury
at a woman whose legs dimple in stretch pants

as she hoists an American flag she's bused-in
to jounce protesting the Islamic Center—

at Chambers my Pakistani fruit vendor's miniature Statue of Liberty
in the mangoes (I say *my)*

has a note taped to the torch:
I AM AMERICAN

(Revenge is an expensive souvenir—)
where does sacred ground

end?
      we live

here   even laughter will not
be forbidden

---

severe clear

9:03 a.m. the people of Flight 175
reach—
I am on my balcony three blocks
away

reaching

Notes Toward an Installation, Jupiter's Theater

A demented civilization forgets

what it has done with its bodies—

Room 1: Cadaver pile projected, clay floor

flickers like an inability to concentrate—

Forgive me seeing you—

as a sack of dirt, eyes open—

Room 2: (Photos) wounds puckering—

(photos) obsidian War Memorials, carved names—

Nothing is the thing itself but the thing—

(thing?)—

Living body, body

in privacy—

Room 3: A burning window frame is labeled EXIT—

Architecture reimagines the body—

Place of Memory—

body connected to everything, despite discontinuity (catalogue says)—

Rooms 4-10: Cadaver piles projected—

and shapely indoor clouds pumped-in (very popular)—

Like Lambs for Sacrifice Our Vaporous Figments

Interrogate Atonement (wall text says). An arrow points

To the Coffee Bar. Visitors leaving Jupiter's Theater—

surprise, no spoilers!—*must Run*—

Made to Disappear, wordless. Worse

than a dream.

... farmers gone;
Crooked sickles beaten into swords.

—Virgil

Sky Notes / Sky Sonnet (3)

Then proclaimed Hnaef   the battle-young king:
'This is not the eastern dawn   nor is a dragon flying here. . . .'

—The Finnsburg Fragment

, Western Sky—streak of light—rocket debris on re-entry
, Beloved days: *remember the good of me*
, our life in latitudes, arc of storyline

, Jupiter in the Summer Triangle, Milky Way dust
, the stars' night-trace of metal from an Old English poem
, glint of spears in the King's feasting hall
, the treacherous King, offering false hospitality

, English is where we meet, trace Latin
, I love, we love, our story
, sun's distance from Time's start

, Today, a way of thinking
, is aimed at someone (offending Kingdom)
, how to end Medieval vengeance?
, in the poem, Danes return to burn the city, swords illumined

Another

Another dog will get a reward, chew splinters
of bone.

Another girl will get hit in the nose—*nothing serious*—
stars on impact. Another.

So much to chew. To hit. At the murdered boy's funeral
a shining baby sucks his own sweet toes—

Time is not finished with children
gunned down.

So much to escape. To fight—. Buried
children like nuclear waste

Crackling under our fields, half-lives
leaking. To leak. To spill. In this country,

Another country. In our ideas, hidden tyranny
of a single idea:

Erase complexity. Pull down each
obdurate thing, small.

Because a lie

is easier

At least, at first. Another lie.

Another. Like the ones we live by _____.

Appetite

no escape from eating
technology extends my appetite

       even books in the library, knowledge
I want to consume   to eat

Whitman read Revelation
tuning its magnitudes to his *concrete divine*
(google Whitman, 1819-1892)
       catalogues sing   I eat   I kiss

   •

on my hungriest Christmas Eve   (loneliness
an inner scraping) *Great Expectations*
miraculously on my iPhone
I am the boy (list all characters named Pip)
who steals a cooling meat pie
from its wooden plank for a convict's meal

       Abundant life from books, TV
internet   mouthful by mouthful   I binge   I eat

   •

information at my fingertips, I mean *fingerprints*

       I eat   I eat

(also to be sipped): my online searches   my e-disposition:

—*The Islamic Dream Book*

—Florida's Yellow Butterflies

—Chaos & Hunger

(Chaos is not not-order but a condition in which
things lose identity…as things)

•

     All
       revolutions exaggerate

Let the strange retain strangeness:

—princess pine in the woods
from Carboniferous, 360 million year reign

—witch hazel's yellow petals like false eyelashes
affixed to branches (best for divining rods)

—dream of a missing tooth in Persia, auguring death of a child

•

I google Revelation   I feast:
—*then I saw a new heaven and a new earth*
—*then he showed me the river of life, bright as crystal*
—*and there shall be no night*
—*and the dogs and sorcerers outside*

for the first heaven & first earth
have passed away   to eat   to be absorbed

                        When I need to prophesy my future
I look into the present, Time's mouth

Wake

The mourners want pleasure
and his blue eyes
Romantic

in the photo with the Christmas tree and a favorite dog
but safely in the past.
Oh, we traveled through his stories—

woolen ditches, taste for the delirious,
his beauty,
a few good parties' flair.

Mourners like to be surprised
(the secrets!—)
to etch a fragmentary person

into a complete work of imagination.
Some people keep falling—
grabbing and falling—

they tire us out. Mourning
like cracked icing on homemade cake.
We eat it up, happy to survive.

Finally, the photo of the last dog in a party hat
is *Sad*—say it with bite
the way he bit into it when we laughed so hard.

Sky Notes / Sky Sonnet (4)

There are signs that men may profit from:
Often at evening we see how various colors
Wander across the face of the setting sun,
And each tells a different story about the future—

—Virgil

, South-South-West, does Venus
, appear, gleaming in her dish of treetops
, Mercury, in chill darkness
, I go outdoors, that I may see myself

, false-dawn, glittering asteroid bits
, crumbs from planets' formation (4.5 billion years ago)
, (illness also) we see through light shards
, comet at the back of his throat, his rebuke—then whisper

, *touch*—is this not, finally, coming to our senses?
, we make our souls
, not far from bears on the orchard trail, apples in their lusty mouths

, the wild of it, this world-sight
, not far from Underground Railroad caves, where bears live
, we make our souls' sequence, love at last sight

Trust

Creator shall I bloom in loveliness plump
as furry bees, round
as cherubim hoisted on wings
chesting into open palms of petals—
pollen; acres of it

bright zags of sound, my bee-fur laden,
pollen-pouches at loading docks.
"I adore pollinators," I confide
as we walk by the river in the real
day—but I mean Sex & Poetry.

Then dream-voices
invite the swarm to my face
to suck grime of years
to renew my youth

—sparkling purr & shuffle
as bees alight on Japanese anemones
(pink petals, heart-filaments pumped open).
And fear

of stings
like punches
at the corners of my eyes & mouth—
are such things possible again? Trust?

Sky Notes / Sky Sonnet (5)

A Bird to overhear
Delight without a Cause—

—Emily Dickinson

, to fetch a pail of water, to fetch Spring

, Spring rushed across his face, seeing me!

, that we become ourselves (& others), whose Body

, even in illness

, I write Dear Friend to say our stars & fire-pour

, magnitude & spectral distance—*his irreducible Self*

, the Ancients saw these stars,—open cluster just below Scorpio's tail

, their Bodies (in us)

, to fetch, to make for each other

, almost to a hollowing, I wish for his escape (also, for myself)

, to listen, to build from the inside

, *finally, we deal with the body*, he says

, at center of the visible

, we sip

Constellation

Bucket I carry—weight & pulse
of a way to think.

Whatever I love
(however I think so)

fluid measure
spills:

my toddler-nephew agitated by lit skyscrapers
points to those gods *outside outside*

each time he wakes.
Insula—whatever is

inside,
(inside) distance between people

upon whom we depend—
their well-being,

need to be free—

Galaxy's

thin blaze

of milk

Sky Notes / Sky Sonnet (6)

Arrestless as invisible—
A matter of the Skies.

—Emily Dickinson

, air-awash, shining particulate—his greeny-eyebeams frozen

, then—Spring rushes across his face, *he sees me*

, Giotto's faces also in tender recognition, Blue skies crackle, oxidizing green

, earth-stuff, materials (we are made of)

, *observable (sometimes) decipherable*, he says

, he helps me look: wind—tiny silver paint-strokes render the under-leaves light

, Time cracks open when we laugh

, world-traveling, my world

, shrinks to a diagnostic calamity—

, but when it happens, it happens: *that feeling alive*

, what is it? a voice whispers— feeling *everything seeing*

, separate also: lucky to care for the Beloved in stable shelter

, to see animals & insects, clouds into wisps

, his radiance (and mine), after all

Distance

Though (if I look) the abandoned
barn magnetizes fear
  & God's dreaded
presence pours
infinite space.

I didn't know you
  once. Sexy &
impatient in your
teenage bed—
room with a sink in the Bronx—

  Time-ago-o (your perfectly
shaped knees). Whatever we are now
this is harvest; galaxies of fruit fall,
distance
closes. Listen.

Notes

Blue Guides derive from the 19th century guidebook tradition. They specialize in art and architecture.

"Blue Guide, Gianicolo" The Aventine and the Gianicolo are among Rome's seven hills. The Priory of Malta on the Aventine, designed by Piranesi, has a keyhole in its garden doorway that frames St. Peter's dome.

"Sky Notes / Sky Sonnet (1)" The first four lines borrow from Walt Whitman's *Specimen Days*, page 105, in Melville House's superb 2014 edition.

"Sky Notes / Sky Sonnet (2)" The opening section, *Sky Notes*, quotes Leo Tolstoy's *War and Peace*, Book 3, Chapter XIX. Richard Pevear and Larissa Volokhonsky, translators.

"Blue Guide: Ruins" Ostia Antica is the archeological site of the ancient port city of Rome.

> *The extensive excavations of the Roman city of Osita Antica are one of the most interesting and beautiful sights near Rome. They are extremely easy to reach from Rome by public transport in half an hour.....the ruins in a beautiful park of umbrella pines and cypresses, give a remarkable idea of the domestic and commercial architecture prevalent in the Empire in the late 1C and 2C AD, hardly any of which has survived in Rome itself, and are as important for the study of Roman urban life as those of older cities of Pompeii and Herculaneum.*

Macadam, Alta. *Blue Guide Rome*. (New York: WW Norton, 2003), page 447.

Lido di Ostia is dotted with old seaside resorts. Ostia Borgo is the modern-day settlement near the archeological site's train station.

"Life as To-Do List"

Before writing was deeply interiorized by print, people did not feel themselves situated every moment of their lives in abstract computed time of any sort. It appears unlikely that most persons in medieval or even Renaissance western Europe would have been aware of the number of the current calendar year—from the birth of Christ or any other point in the past. Why should they be? . . . In a culture with no newspapers or other currently dated material to impinge on consciousness, what would be the point for most people in knowing the current calendar year? The abstract calendar number would be related to nothing in real life. Most persons did not know and never even tried to discover in what calendar year they were born.

Walter Ong. *Orality and Literacy: Technologizing the Word* (New York: Routledge, 1982), pages 97-98.

"Face of North America"   Farb, Peter. *Face of North America: The Natural History of a Continent.* New York: Harper & Row, 1968.

Italicized lines from the sections entitled "Face of North America" quote Farb, in some cases with minor changes for compression.

Many resources about Heart Mountain are now available online at www.heartmountain.org, the website of the organization that maintains the physical camp, now a center for learning.

www.encyclopedia.densho.org links to the archives of Heart Mountain history, including the Loyalty Questionnaire; Frank Emi's correspondence (one of the organizers of the Heart Mountain Fairness Committee); and other documents produced by The Fairness Committee, et al.

"Exclusion Zone"   In Lower Manhattan in 2010, there was an attempt to prevent development of an Islamic community center near the former World Trade Towers. Community Board 1 of Manhattan bravely refused an Exclusion Zone and would not ban the project (May 25, 2010), though the center was not built.

"Another" *Stanley Kunitz typescript: "Poetry opposes the tyranny of a single idea."*

"Appetite" With thanks to Miriam Nichols for her lecture "Mythopoesis in Charles Olson's Later *Maximus Poems:* The Importance of the Beautiful" presented on December 4, 2014 at the School of Visual Arts, sponsored by the MFA Program in Art Criticism & Writing. Quotations from the Book of Revelation are from the Revised Standard Version.

Thank you to brilliant David Ferry for epigraph translations of Virgil and Horace.

Acknowledgments

Warm acknowledgment is made to the editors of the following magazines, in which some of these poems first appeared:

The Cortland Review; Ploughshares; Still Against War III, Poems for Marie Ponsot; Still Against War V, Poems for Marie Ponsot; and *Women's Voices for Change.*

I am grateful to my family, friends, and colleagues for their support during the writing of this book. Special thanks to Carol Conroy for her close readings. Additional thanks to: Elizabeth Arnold, Catherine Barnett, Genine Lentine, Marnie Mueller, Naomi Shihab Nye, Jane Preston, Martha Rhodes, Thomas Sleigh, and the team at Four Way Books.

Publication of this book was made possible by grants and donations. We are also grateful to those individuals who participated in our 2017 Build a Book Program. They are:

Anonymous (6), Evan Archer, Sally Ball, Jan Bender-Zanoni, Zeke Berman, Kristina Bicher, Laurel Blossom, Carol Blum, Betsy Bonner, Mary Brancaccio, Lee Briccetti, Deirdre Brill, Anthony Cappo, Carla & Steven Carlson, Caroline Carlson, Stephanie Chang, Tina Chang, Liza Charlesworth, Maxwell Dana, Machi Davis, Marjorie Deninger, Lukas Fauset, Monica Ferrell, Emily Flitter, Jennifer Franklin, Martha Webster & Robert Fuentes, Chuck Gillett, Dorothy Goldman, Dr. Lauri Grossman, Naomi Guttman & Jonathan Mead, Steven Haas, Mary Heilner, Hermann Hesse, Deming Holleran, Nathaniel Hutner, Janet Jackson, Christopher Kempf, David Lee, Jen Levitt, Howard Levy, Owen Lewis, Paul Lisicky, Sara London & Dean Albarelli, David Long, Katie Longofono, Cynthia Lowen, Ralph & Mary Ann Lowen, Donna Masini, Louise Mathias, Catherine McArthur, Nathan McClain, Gregory McDonald, Britt Melewski, Kamilah Moon, Carolyn Murdoch, Rebecca & Daniel Okrent, Tracey Orick, Zachary Pace, Gregory Pardlo, Allyson Paty, Marcia & Chris Pelletiere, Taylor Pitts, Eileen Pollack, Barbara Preminger, Kevin Prufer, Vinode Ramgopal, Martha Rhodes, Roni & Richard Schotter, Peter & Jill Schireson, Soraya Shalforoosh, Peggy Shinner, James Snyder & Krista Fragos, Megan Staffel, Alice St. Claire-Long, Robin Taylor, Marjorie & Lew Tesser, Boris Thomas, Judith Thurman, Susan Walton, Calvin Wei, Abby Wender, Bill Wenthe, Allison Benis White, Elizabeth Whittlesey, Hao Wu, Monica Youn, and Leah Zander.